# DOG CARE

OY SCOUTS OF AMERICA
RVING, TEXAS

# Requirements

1. Tell some of the characteristics of 10 breeds of dogs, OR give a short history of one.
2. Point out on a dog (or on a sketch) at least 10 parts. Give the correct name of each.
3. Present a report signed by a parent or guardian describing the care you have given your dog for 2 months. Include these items: feeding schedule, food used, housing, exercising, grooming, and bathing. Tell what has been done to keep the dog alert and healthy.
4. Present a written report showing about how much it costs to keep your dog for 2 months.
5. Explain the right way to obedience train. Show with your dog any three of these commands: "Come," "Sit," "Down," "Heel," "Stay," "Take it," "Drop it," "Get it."
6. Do at least TWO of the following:
   a. Describe what should be done to remove fleas, ticks, and lice from your dog.
   b. Describe the symptoms of the following: distemper, rabies, mange, ringworm. Explain what you would do if your dog showed these.
   c. Describe the proper treatment for sore ear, sore eye, fits, removing something swallowed by a dog, removing something stuck in its throat.
   d. Explain first aid for a dogbite. List the things needed in every dog owner's first aid kit.
7. Explain precautions to take in handling a hurt dog. Show how to put on an emergency muzzle. Explain how to treat wounds. Show how to put on a simple dressing and bandage the foot, body, or head. Explain what to do if a dog is hit by a car.
8. Tell the dangers of home treatment of a serious ailment. Report on a visit to a veterinary hospital; or report on a visit to an animal shelter.
9. Know the laws and ordinances involving dogs in force in your town.

33289
ISBN 0-8395-3289-X
©1984 Boy Scouts of America
1999 Printing of the 1984 Revision

# Contents

Dogs have been bred for many purposes, resulting in a variety of shapes, sizes, and special features. The pair of Pekingese, *above,* are small with snub noses and long, silky coats. They were originally bred in China as house pets. The basset hound, *right,* is smooth-coated and muscular with a long muzzle and a keen sense of smell. These hounds were originally bred in Germany to track game.

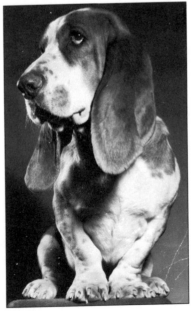

# Dog Breeds and Features

About 40 million years ago there lived a small meat-eating animal that had short legs and a long tail and looked something like a civet cat. Scientists believe this creature was the ancient forebear of the wolf and of wild dogs. The earliest dogs probably resembled the present-day dingo, the wild dog of Australia. Hunting together in packs, wolves and wild dogs roamed fields and forests in prehistoric times, filling the nights with their lonely howls.

Dogs probably were the first animals to be domesticated. Prehistoric humans living in the Stone Age about 12,000 years ago tamed the wild dog and made it a companion, draft animal, and sentry. We know from the evidence left behind by these early people in their camps and burial mounds that they kept dogs, probably as hunters and trackers and to act as watchdogs. Later, as humans began to raise sheep, cattle, and other livestock, their dogs learned to herd the flocks and watch over them. In the temples and tombs of ancient civilizations, drawings and inscriptions show that the ancient Egyptians (5000 B.C.) kept short-legged house dogs and tall spotted dogs that looked like greyhounds. The saluki also was kept; it is the oldest recognized breed. The Assyrians (700 B.C.) used a powerful mastiff type of dog for hunting.

## In America

When the first explorers came from Europe to America, they discovered that American Indians also kept dogs. These animals not only served as watchdogs and pets, but also as beasts of burden, drawing the *travois,* a stretcher-like sled made of two branches that were dragged along the ground.

## Ancestors of Various Breeds

The wolf is the ancestor of the modern domestic dog. All wolves, and foxes as well, are canines and can interbreed with dogs and produce completely normal pups.

The different dog breeds were created by humans using selective breeding through the ages to get the qualities they wanted. Some dogs were bred to hunt, some to serve as guard or sled dogs, and some to be herders. Others were kept as pets, companions, and guides.

The wolflike wild dogs that lived millions of years ago gave way, as the centuries passed, to certain definite modern breeds. Scientists believe four major types of dogs existed in Europe by 3500 B.C. One may have been the ancestor of such powerful dogs as German shepherds, huskies, and chow chows. Another type was a primitive sheepdog from which sheepdogs and collies were derived, and another was a small dog from which terriers and Pomeranians later developed. A fourth type probably was the ancestor of most hounds, except perhaps the greyhound, which may have developed directly from the original dingo-like wild dog.

## Breeds of Dogs

Dog breeds vary tremendously in shape, size, color, and characteristics. Some have been bred and made official quite recently, while others are just about the same today as when they were pictured on Egyptian and Assyrian tombs and monuments thousands of years ago.

The American Kennel Club recognizes 128 of the more than 400 breeds of dogs found worldwide. You won't be expected to learn them all as you earn this merit badge, but you should know the main groupings of the dog family and be able to recognize several different breeds. Some are common; you have probably seen them often. Others are rare and will seldom be seen outside of dog shows.

The AKC divides dog breeds into seven groups, which are based on the uses for which the breeds were originally developed. They are Sporting, Hound, Working, Terrier, Toy, Non-Sporting, and Herding.

## Breed Characteristics

One or two interesting breeds from each of the groups are described and illustrated here.

**English Setter.** This beautiful silky-haired hunting dog is noted for its intelligence in the field. Colors range from black, tan, and white to solid white. The setter is a gentle dog, but, since it weighs 50 pounds or more, is more suited to the country than the city. Under a

# BREEDS OF DOGS

ELIGIBLE FOR REGISTRATION IN
AMERICAN KENNEL CLUB STUD BOOK

## SPORTING GROUP
Brittanys
Pointers
Pointers, German
  Shorthaired
Pointers, German
  Wirehaired
Retrievers, Chesapeake
  Bay
Retrievers, Curly-Coated
Retrievers, Flat-Coated
Retrievers, Golden
Retrievers, Labrador
Setters, English
Setters, Gordon
Setters, Irish
Spaniels, American Water
Spaniels, Clumber
Spaniels, Cocker
Spaniels, English Cocker
Spaniels, English Springer
Spaniels, Field
Spaniels, Irish Water
Spaniels, Sussex
Spaniels, Welsh Springer
Vizslas
Weimaraners
Wirehaired Pointed
  Griffons

## HOUND GROUP
Afghan Hounds
Basenjis
Basset Hounds
Beagles
Black & Tan Coonhounds
Bloodhounds
Borzois
Dachshunds
Foxhounds, American
Foxhounds, English
Greyhounds
Harriers
Ibizan Hounds
Irish Wolfhounds
Norwegian Elkhounds
Otter Hounds
Rhodesian Ridgebacks
Salukis
Scottish Deerhounds
Whippets

## WORKING GROUP
Akitas
Alaskan Malamutes
Bernese Mountain Dogs
Boxers
Bullmastiffs
Doberman Pinschers
Giant Schnauzers
Great Danes
Great Pyrenees
Komondorok
Kuvaszok
Mastiffs
Newfoundlands
Rottweilers
St. Bernards
Samoyeds
Siberian Huskies
Standard Schnauzers

## TERRIER GROUP
Airedale Terriers
American Staffordshire
  Terriers
Australian Terriers
Bedlington Terriers
Border Terriers
Bull Terriers
Cairn Terriers
Dandie Dinmont Terriers
Fox Terriers
Irish Terriers
Kerry Blue Terriers
Lakeland Terriers
Manchester Terriers
Miniature Schnauzers
Norfolk Terriers
Norwich Terriers
Scottish Terriers
Sealyham Terriers
Skye Terriers
Soft-Coated Wheaten
  Terriers
Staffordshire Bull
  Terriers
Welsh Terriers

West Highland White

## TOY GROUP
Affenpinschers
Brussels Griffons
Chihuahuas
English Toy Spaniels
Italian Greyhounds
Japanese Chin
Maltese
Manchester Terriers
Miniature Pinschers
Papillons
Pekingese
Pomeranians
Poodles (Toy)
Pugs
Shih Tzu
Silky Terriers
Yorkshire Terriers

## NON-SPORTING GROUP
Bichons Frises
Boston Terriers
Bulldogs
Chow Chows
Dalmatians
French Bulldogs
Keeshonden
Lhasa Apsos
Poodles
Schipperkes
Tibetan Terriers

## HERDING GROUP
Australian Cattle Dogs
Bearded Collies
Belgian Malinois
Belgian Sheepdogs
Belgian Tervuren
Bouviers des Flandres
Briards
Collies
German Shepherd Dogs
Old English Sheepdogs
Pulik
Shetland Sheepdogs
Welsh Corgis, Cardigan
Welsh Corgis, Pembroke

good trainer this dog shows remarkable skill as a gun dog in field trials.

**Pointer.** The pointer is a large sporting dog, weighing 50 to 60 pounds. Its short coat is usually white, with black or yellow markings. Developed in England more than 300 years ago, it hunts game birds by scent. It stands rigidly poised with its nose facing the game, directing the hunter to it. Its size and breeding make it a better country dog than city dog.

**Beagle.** This small, compact hound weighs 20 to 40 pounds. Its short, close-lying, harsh coat usually is black, tan, and white. Developed in England to hunt hares, it was introduced into the U.S. in the 1870s. It is an obedient and friendly dog.

**Dachshund.** This small, short-legged hound, weighing 5 to 20 pounds, is black or chocolate with tan, or may have a solid red coat. Varieties include smooth-haired, longhaired, wire-haired, and miniatures of each. The breed was developed in Germany over hundreds of years to hunt badgers. It will go into a badger's burrow and fight with great courage until its master is able to dig the badger out.

**Boxer.** This medium-sized, muscular working dog has a short, smooth coat of fawn or brindle, often with white markings. First used for fighting, the breed originated in 16th century Europe and was perfected in 19th century Germany. It weighs about 65 pounds.

**Airedale Terrier.** A large terrier, the Airedale weighs 40 to 50 pounds. Its dense, wiry, close-lying coat is a mixture of tan, black, and grizzle. The breed probably was produced from crosses of the extinct black-and-tan terrier and the otterhound. It can dive into deep water, competing with a retriever on even terms. It is noted for loyalty and courage and makes an excellent guardian of children.

**Fox Terrier.** There are two types —the smooth, with a dense, short, flat coat, and the wirehaired, with a longer, harsh, wiry coat. Both are long-legged terriers weighing 15 to 19 pounds, and are white, with black or black-and-tan markings. The breed was perfected in 19th century England to hunt foxes. The smooth-haired terrier is an excellent house pet because of its alert good nature, small size, and short coat.

**Pekingese.** This popular toy dog, weighing from 1½ (toy size) to 15 pounds, has for remote ancestors the Egyptian house dog and later the Chinese lion dog. History records that the emperors of China considered this breed their personal property and therefore sacred. Its long, soft coat, which may be any color, forms a ruff around the neck.

**Pomeranian.** A sturdy toy dog weighing 3 to 7 pounds, the Pomeranian has an abundant double coat that forms a ruff on the neck. Descended from the larger sled dogs of Iceland and Lapland, it became popular when Queen Victoria obtained one in the late 19th century. It makes an excellent watchdog. Small as it is, it sounds a lively alarm if any prowler appears.

**Boston Terrier.** A small, lively non-sporting dog, the Boston terrier weighs 13 to 25 pounds and is one of the few dog breeds native to the U.S. Its short, smooth coat may be brindle or black, with white markings. Good natured, it is playful and fond of children. Its intelligence, courage, rather small size, and short coat make it an ideal house dog.

**Dalmatian.** This hardy non-sporting dog is known for speed and endurance. It weighs 35 to 50 pounds, and has a short, glossy coat, white with black or dark-brown spots. In horsedrawn fire engine days, Dalmatians were often seen running behind the equipment, sometimes in pairs. The Dalmatian is still popular as a pet of the firehouse. It was bred as a fashionable coach dog, and is happiest where it can get plenty of outdoor exercise.

**German Shepherd.** This large, muscular herding dog weighs 60 to 85 pounds. It has a dense undercoat and a harsh outercoat that usually is black, gray, or black and tan. Developed as a sheepherder and perfected in Germany about 1900, it has been used in war, in police work, and as a guide dog for the blind.

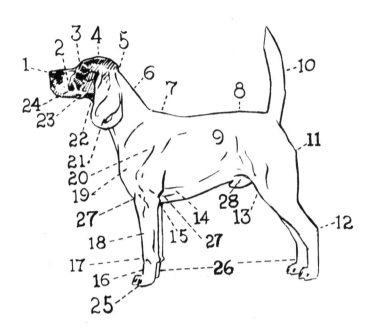

## Parts of a Dog

The illustration shows parts of the dog, properly named. Many of these terms will be familiar to you, and others will be new. They are the terms used by judges in dog shows and are known to all experts.

1. Nose
2. Muzzle
3. Stop
4. Skull
5. Occiput
6. Arch or crest
7. Withers or top of shoulders
8. Hip
9. Loin
10. Brush, flag, or tail
11. Point of rump
12. Hock or tarsus
13. Stifle or knee
14. Chest
15. Elbow
16. Pastern or metacarpus
17. Carpus or wrist
18. Forearm
19. Point of shoulder
20. Shoulder
21. Ear or leather
22. Dewlap
23. Lips or flews
24. Cheek
25. Toes or digits
26. Dewclaws
27. Brisket
28. Sheath

# Selecting and Caring for a Dog

Before you get a dog, think about how your pet will affect those around you. Is your family as interested in having one as you are? Can someone take care of your dog when you go camping and are away for a week? Talk with other family members—perhaps even your neighbors or landlord—before you buy or adopt any dog.

What kind of dog should you get? Your choice will depend mainly on what you want the dog for and where you live. Perhaps you need a watchdog in a city home. Maybe you want a hunting dog. You may live on a farm and need a stock dog. If you live in the country or on the outskirts of town, you may have room for a large dog. If you live in an apartment or deep in the heart of a big city, a small dog might be a better choice.

Consider the expense of keeping a dog. Can you afford to feed a Great Dane, or can you better afford to feed a terrier? A big dog eats more, costs more, and will need more exercise.

Should you get a puppy or an older dog? A new puppy is a delight but it must be housebroken and trained to obey basic commands. Usually the extra trouble of early training will be repaid by the mutual bond of understanding and devotion that develops between dog and master as the puppy grows up. Older dogs may become homesick, and they may have bad habits or earlier loyalties that are hard to change. However, an older animal probably will be housebroken and already trained in the basics of obedience.

What breed do you want? Purebred dogs generally will have been carefully bred and lovingly cared for. They may be entered in dog shows and they have a certain guarantee of worth. Mixed breed dogs are just as loyal and intelligent as purebred animals and just as much fun. A mixed breed dog has the advantage of costing far less than most purebreds. If you decide to get a mixed breed dog, be sure the animal has not been neglected or mistreated.

Think about whether you want a dog with long hair or short hair. A long-haired dog will shed hair on rugs and furniture and will need frequent grooming, while a short-haired dog is easier to keep clean and well groomed and doesn't create as much of a housekeeping problem.

Do you want a male or a female dog? Unless you have her spayed, a female will go through a breeding period twice a year and must be kept away from males for about 3 weeks during that time. In spite of this, a female is as good a pet as a male, and perhaps more so. Many experts believe that females are less likely to stray or to fight other dogs. Certainly there's no truth to the idea that a male dog is any more or any less intelligent or friendly than a female.

Unless your pet is a valuable breeding or show dog, it's recommended that you have females spayed and males neutered. Spaying will prevent females from coming into season, and neutering will lessen a male dog's desire to roam and to fight with other males. The operation should be discussed with your veterinarian, who can advise you on how old your dog should be when the surgery is done.

## Buying Your Dog

Puppies are old enough to leave their mother's care when they are from 6 to 8 weeks old. Make sure the puppy you've chosen is fully weaned and strong enough to be on its own away from its mother. The puppy should be healthy, normal, and alert. Avoid a listless dog, one that coughs or has a runny nose, watery eyes, skin rashes, or seems to be running a temperature. Check under the ears and thighs for insect bites. Test for deafness by clapping your hands and for lameness by watching the puppy walk. Avoid a cowering, trembling puppy, or one that seems snappy and ill-tempered. Always select a lively puppy, not necessarily the largest or smallest of the litter. If you don't intend to show the animal, you often can save money by buying a "pet quality" puppy.

It is recommended that you buy from a person who has a female with a litter of healthy pups. However, excellent dogs are sometimes available from a reliable kennel or pet store, or from the SPCA, animal rescue leagues, or similar organizations.

When you get a dog, find out what inoculations have been given and when. Find out what feeding schedule the pup is on. Get as much medical history as possible. With this information, take the dog to a veterinarian for advice as to current care and inoculations and future requirements. A veterinarian can tell you if the pup needs deworming or "shots."

If the dog is American Kennel Club registered, be sure to get the registration papers at the time of purchase. A copy of the animal's pedigree usually is furnished by the seller; however, if the information is not available at the time of purchase, you can buy a copy from the American Kennel Club, 51 Madison Avenue, New York, NY 10010.

## Housing Your Dog

Transport the puppy in a well-ventilated, leakproof box and install your pet in its new sleeping box or basket without undue excitement. The basket should be raised off the floor several inches to avoid drafts and dampness. Spread an old blanket or towel in the bed to make it comfortable and keep your puppy warm at night. After the puppy is housebroken, a washable pad or cushion may be placed in the bed.

Don't use a wicker basket for a puppy's bed. The animal may chew on the basket and accidentally swallow some of the splinters.

Be careful not to tire out the new arrival; a puppy tires easily. Don't let younger children play roughly with the pup, as too much excitement and play may cause illness.

All dogs except toy breeds can sleep outdoors under proper conditions, but avoid sudden changes in temperature. A garage or barn makes a good shelter for the sleeping box. Avoid concrete floors because they are damp. Make sure the bed is away from drafts. An outdoor kennel should be weatherproof with the floor raised above the ground. It should have a cozy sleeping compartment or bed.

The dog's bedding should be cleaned and replaced from time to time. Flea powder may be sprinkled into the bedding occasionally. If it's kept outdoors, the dog's sleeping compartment should be small enough to retain the dog's body heat. An old blanket may be included for extra warmth as needed.

## Crying at Night

A new puppy may whine or cry at night because it is lonesome or cold. If this happens, be sure that the sleeping box is warm enough. Sometimes an old slipper, a hot-water bottle (not hot enough to burn), or a ticking clock will help comfort the puppy the first few nights.

## Housebreaking

A puppy may have been "paper broken" in a kennel. If so, place a folded newspaper near your pet's bed. Put the puppy on this after each meal until it gets used to the paper and will go to it. Leave a small piece of soiled paper there as a hint that this is the place. Do not water the puppy at night.

Some trainers recommend the use of commercial "piddle pads" instead of newspaper. With newspaper there is the possibility of urine seepage and having the pet's scent left on the floor. If you do use newspaper, you may wish to place a plastic sheet underneath to protect the floor.

If a puppy has had no training, surround the area near its bed with paper or piddle pads and put your pet on the same section after each feeding. Move this farther and farther away from the bed until the puppy learns to use it in the corner of the room. Patience, kindness, and high praise are essential during this phase of a puppy's training.

Once a puppy is paper trained, take it outdoors for a while every morning as soon as it wakes. Do this after each feeding and just before bedtime. Always take the puppy out by the same door repeating the question, "Want to go out?" Keep your pet off the main sidewalk, following the well-known rule, "Curb your dog!" Take along a "pooper-scooper," or an ordinary plastic bag, to help you in cleaning up after your dog. (Put the bag over your hand like a mitten, pick up the dog's mess with your covered hand, turn the bag inside out, close it, and throw it away.) Always take the dog over the same route; dogs are creatures of habit. When the puppy gets the idea, which may take a week or 10 days, it will go to the door when it is ready and bark to go out.

If the puppy makes a mistake during this period, scold your pet at the time and take it outside. Always remember that you must correct the animal while it is doing something wrong or immediately afterward for it to understand why it's being scolded. Rubbing a puppy's nose in it won't help much. A loud "no!" with a clap of your hands works best to discourage the wrong behavior.

Many trainers caution against the use of physical punishment to discipline a dog, such as pushing the dog or hitting it on the rump with a folded newspaper. Vocal reprimand—saying "no!" and scolding the dog—is your best course of action. Never whip a dog or rap it on the nose, as this can cause a dog to fear hands and turn into a "fear biter." Hitting your pet is more likely to get you a frightened, nervous animal than a well-behaved one.

Always praise a dog and pet it when it does what you want. This is very important. When you scold your dog for the wrong behavior, be sure to then show it what the right behavior is. Pets generally want to please their owners and will learn good behavior if you show them what to do gently, consistently, and patiently.

## Chewing Things

Dogs naturally like to bite and chew things. Furnish your pup with a hard pet-shop dog bone, a stuffed bag, a rag doll, or knotted cloth to chew on. These are considered the dog's personal property to treat as it pleases. If the puppy bites the wrong things, scold the animal at once and give one of the toys to play with instead. The puppy will learn in time which things are okay to play with and which things aren't. Don't give chew toys that look like items found around the house, for puppies and many adult dogs can't tell the difference between the toys and the look-alike items that they're supposed to leave alone.

**Dogs should be given toys of their own to chew on and taught not to chew on items found in the house.**

# Exercise

Dogs need exercise to remain in good health. The larger the dog the more exercise it needs. Both walking and roaming around for pleasure are required for proper exercise of your dog.

If you live in a suburban or rural area, you may be able to fence off an area where your dog can run and play. In the city, exercise for your dog becomes more of a problem. You'll have to take your pet out for walks. A large dog such as a Great Dane may need a 2-hour hike each day to stay fit, while a small dog will do all right with a couple of strolls daily. If your dog is not properly exercised, it will become fat, lazy, and subject to sickness.

Keep your pet on a leash, especially in areas where traffic is heavy. Some cities require dogs to be on a leash at all times. Make sure the collar and leash are not too heavy. Get the dog used to wearing the collar and leash gradually over short periods.

Several short walks each day are recommended for a puppy. Avoid violent play or excessive handling by younger children.

**All dogs need varying amounts of exercise to remain in good health.**

# Grooming

Too much bathing is not good for a dog. Puppies under the age of 3 months should generally not be bathed. A good daily grooming or a cleaning with a damp washcloth is sufficent for them. Don't bathe a dog more often than once a month, unless your pet gets into the mud or some other mess and really has to have a bath to come clean.

**Long-haired dogs require frequent grooming.**

Don't use a soap or shampoo meant for humans; it's probably too harsh for a dog's skin. Use warm—never hot or cold—water. Put wads of cotton in the ears and, with help, several drops of heavy mineral oil in the eyes before the bath. Keep soap and water out of the ears and eyes. Rinse thoroughly, more than once if necessary, so that no soap is left on the skin. Rinse with lukewarm water, not cold.

Dry your dog thoroughly after every bath, since a dog can easily catch cold. Use heavy towels and keep your pet warm and away from drafts until thoroughly dry.

Between baths, brush and groom your dog. If you have a short-haired dog, give it a rubdown with a soft cloth or piece of chamois. Long-haired dogs will require grooming every day or two with a wide-toothed comb and a brush with long bristles. Spread a newspaper on a table to catch the combings and place the dog on the paper. Work from head to tail. Talk to your pet during the grooming, and it will probably be a pleasant experience for both of you. Follow the brushing with a rubdown, using a soft cloth.

If the dog has fleas, you may want to dust its coat and skin with flea powder after the grooming. On a young pup, however, the use of a chemical may be dangerous. The animal could lick it off. Check with your veterinarian for safe ways to rid your dog of fleas. (See the section on external parasites under "Dog Illnesses.")

## Toenails

It is not true that because dogs wear down their toenails running and walking, they do not need pedicures. Overgrown toenails—unfortunately common among household dogs—can actually warp a dog's foot and leg structure by forcing the dog to walk painfully "around" its nails on its pasterns—like human beings walking on their ankles. Every dog's weekly grooming should include trimming the nails. Pet shops sell special files you can use to shorten your dog's nails. For longer nails, use a nail clipper, with great care. Clip the points of the nails only, then file them smooth.

## Cleaning Ears and Eyes

Clean the dog's ears once or twice a month, using your fingertip and cotton balls (not swabs) soaked with rubbing alcohol. Wipe all the nooks and crannies you can see, taking care not to push wax and dirt into the ear canal. Be very gentle; dogs' ears are tender.

Eye care is especially important for breeds with protruding eyes, such as cocker spaniels, Lhasa apsos, and Pekingese. If the dog is prone to an eye discharge, wipe it off daily with water-soaked cotton. Heavy eye discharge may be a sign of disease and should be checked by your veterinarian.

## Clipping and Plucking

This is not a job for an amateur. Kennels, pet shops, and animal hospitals have clipping and plucking services. If your dog is long-haired and needs this service, get the advice of an expert regarding the best procedure.

## Proper Feeding

Today it is very easy to feed your dog a properly balanced diet. Commercial dog foods sold in markets are used by most dog owners, and are recommended by veterinarians. Choose a complete and balanced commercial dog food and feed according to the instructions. Avoid all-meat products and tidbits from the table. Milk, vegetables, cereal, eggs, or other supplements are not needed unless the dog has a special health problem.

Although protein in some form is a dog's basic diet, it is not the only nutrient needed for good health. Carbohydrates, fats, vitamins, and minerals also are part of a balanced diet. By feeding your dog a good commercial food, you can be sure your pet is well nourished. Giving a dog treats from the table not only encourages begging at the table, a bad habit, but also may upset the nutrient balance of the dog's diet.

The amount your pet needs will depend on its individual requirements. Just as some people need to eat more than others, some dogs will require more food than others. Adjust the amount you feed according to the dog's general condition and level of activity.

When you bring a new puppy home, it will already have been started on a diet schedule. Be sure to obtain directions for feeding from the previous owner. Do not change the pup's schedule when you first get it home. Sudden changes often cause intestinal upsets. Any changes should be made gradually. Milk or overfeeding can cause diarrhea.

Puppies must be fed often and in small amounts. As the dog gets older, the number of meals is reduced and the quantity at each meal is increased. From 3 to 6 months, feed a dog four times a day, at morning, noon, afternoon, and evening. From 6 to 9 months, feed three times a day, eliminating the afternoon meal. After a dog is 9 months old, cut back to morning and evening meals. Dogs 1 year and older may do fine on one meal a day. All the leading brands of prepared dog food may be used safely.

This dachshund displays indications of good health.

## Water

Plenty of fresh water should be available for your dog at all times. Use a clean bowl or other container and place it in the shade or where it will stay cool.

## Amount to Feed Daily

The following are estimates for you to use as general guidelines. Adjust the amount according to your dog's needs and the instructions on the dog food package.

| | Dog's weight (lbs.) | Dry meal moistened with water | Semimoist products burgers | packets | Cans |
|---|---|---|---|---|---|
| Growing puppy | 3–5 | 1 cup | 1–2 | 1 | ½ |
| (Total amount | 8–10 | 2–3 cups | 2–3 | 2 | ½–1 |
| is divided into | 15–20 | 4–5 cups | 3–4 | 3 | 1–2 |
| several feedings, | | | | | |
| depending on the | | | | | |
| puppy's age.) | | | | | |
| Adult dog | 20 | 2–2½ cups | 2–3 | 2–3 | 1 |
| (Feed once or | 40 | 4–5 cups | 3–5 | 3–5 | 2–3 |
| twice a day.) | | | | | |

## Don'ts in Dog Feeding

Do not feed a dog pork bones, chicken bones, chop bones, T-bones, or other bones that can splinter. They can cause serious injury. You can give your dog a knuckle bone to chew on, which does not splinter, or a dog toy that is solid enough that your pet can't chew it up and swallow it.

## Factors of Good Health

A dog that is slender, alert, active, and good natured with clear eyes and a glossy coat has the indications of good health. Proper feeding, good housing, plenty of exercise, kind treatment, regular grooming, and a medical checkup will do much to ensure that your dog stays healthy.

# Forms to Use for Merit Badge

The following forms are recommended for use in qualifying for the Dog Care merit badge. They are simple and will help you understand and comply with the merit badge requirements.

## Statement on Dog Care

I CERTIFY that Scout _____ has, over a period of at least 2 months, provided properly for his dog or one under his care, including the following areas:

☐ Feeding schedule
☐ Kinds and amounts of food
☐ Housing
☐ Exercise
☐ Grooming
☐ Health needs

_____ Parent or Guardian
(Signature)

## Report on Feeding and Care of My Dog

Date I started_____ Present date_____
Weight of dog_____ Age of dog_____ Breed_____
Sources of food (purchased dog food, table scraps, other)_____
_____
Estimated average cost per week: $_____
When fed_____a.m. _____p.m.
Veterinary care, if any: When_____
What for_____
Cost $_____
Grooming, how often_____
Bathing, describe_____
Schedule of exercise_____
_____
Signature of Scout:_____

# Responsible Dog Ownership

Every year, millions of puppies and kittens are born in the United States. Many of them will never find a home. Litters of unwanted animals are dumped along roadsides. Dogs and cats are left behind when their owners move or tire of caring for them.

The Humane Society of the United States estimates that 15 to 17 million dogs and cats are turned in to the nation's animal shelters each year. Only about 20 percent of them are adopted or claimed by their owners. The rest—more than 13 million animals a year—are put to death because no one wants them. Additional millions of abandoned animals never even make it to a shelter, where they at least have a chance to be adopted. Instead, they spend their short and miserable lives roaming city streets and country roads. Most of them die from starvation, disease, freezing, or under the wheels of cars.

You can help solve the terrible problem of pet overpopulation and prevent the tragic deaths of millions of unwanted animals yearly. The first thing to do is to be a responsible dog owner. Don't buy or adopt a dog unless you understand the commitment involved and are sure that you'll be able to take care of your pet properly. You must be willing to feed, exercise, groom, and otherwise spend time with your pet according to the dog's needs, not your own convenience.

People who leave a dog shut up alone in an apartment or house for long periods and neglect to feed or exercise it regularly wind up with a frustrated, lonely, badly behaved animal instead of the affectionate companion they wanted. It's these kinds of animals that often are abandoned or taken to a shelter to be put to sleep. Be sure you understand that when you bring a dog into your home, it becomes your responsibility. You have an obligation to care for the animal throughout its lifetime.

You should also plan to have your dog spayed or neutered. Dogs and cats that are allowed to breed freely are at the root of the pet overpopulation problem. If you let your dog breed, you may be able to find homes for that litter. But what happens when each of the puppies has a litter? And when each of those animals produces more litters? Counting all its descendants, one dog can add hundreds or even thousands of new animals to the pet surplus during its lifetime.

There are many advantages to having your dog neutered or spayed. Spaying a female will make her less likely to get mammary cancers, which account for half of all cancers suffered by dogs. Spaying will keep packs of barking males from invading your yard when your female dog is in heat.

A male that has been neutered has less desire to roam, is less aggressive, and tends to be gentler and more affectionate. Your pet won't get in fights as much. He won't be as likely to wander off and get lost or hurt. Neutering will not make dogs fat and lazy, as people commonly believe. Overeating and lack of exercise do that. Neutering will in fact help your pet live a longer and healthier life, and will give you a more affectionate and manageable dog.

Some animal shelters automatically neuter the pets they release for adoption for a small fee, or free. Some veterinarians offer spaying services at reduced rates in cooperation with local humane societies. Unless yours is a valuable breeding animal, there's really no reason not to have your dog spayed or neutered. All things considered, it's best to let the professionals do the breeding. If you do breed your dog, do so only under the supervision of a veterinarian or your counselor.

As a dog-owner, you are responsible not only to your pet, but also to your community. Always clean up after your dog during walks in all places, public or private.

## Owner's Guide *

- License your pet according to your local laws and have it wear an ID tag at all times.
- Keep your pet leashed or under control for its own safety and to keep it from being a nuisance.
- Spay or neuter your pet for its own health and to help curb the dog and cat population explosion in our country.
- Give your pet a nutritious diet, plenty of exercise, and proper veterinary care with vaccinations, including a rabies shot to protect the community.
- Keep your pet in your home, train it patiently, and give it lots of love and attention.

---

* Courtesy of The Humane Society of the United States, Washington, DC 20037.

With patience and
consistency, a dog owner
can train an animal to be a
well-behaved companion.

# Training Your Dog

Some dogs are canine friends to the whole neighborhood, beloved by everyone, while others are considered a nuisance, disliked and avoided. You can prevent your pet from being a community problem dog with a moderate amount of training.

Here are the minimum training requirements considered essential by most experts:

1. To be housebroken
2. To know its name and to respond to the command "come"
3. To go along sensibly on a leash
4. To be free from bad habits such as jumping on people, chasing cars, and barking at night
5. To "heel" on command
6. To "sit" on command
7. To understand and obey the word "no"
8. To understand and obey the commands "down" and "stay"

These are the foundations of canine courtesy.

## The Dog Trainer's Pledge *

I will always be kind to my dog.
I will always play fair with my dog.
I will always be patient when teaching my dog.
I will always try again tomorrow.

## When to Start Training

As soon as you get a puppy, start housebreaking training. Housebreaking is the first step in teaching a dog what you expect of it.

At 3 to 6 months of age, or even earlier, you can begin to train a puppy to walk on a leash. A puppy can start to learn right away such things as its name, your approval expressed by a pat, and the meaning of the word "no." Correct any bad habits early. At 6 to 8 months you can begin more serious training.

---

*From 31 Tricks for Your Dog, by Karlis Petersons, world-famous dog trainer of Ringling Brothers and Barnum and Bailey Circus. Reprinted courtesy Armour and Co., Chicago, IL. 60609.

## How Often?

Short daily periods of training are most effective. Start with 10 minutes and gradually increase the time. Always train before feeding, or wait until 2 hours after a meal.

Teach one trick at a time, and review those already learned before going to a new one. Always praise your dog when it does the right thing, and scold or say "no!" if it does something wrong. Reward successful completion of a training stunt with some bit of food and let your dog know you are pleased.

## Words and Action

When you give your dog a command, make some motion with your hand at the same time and always use the same word and motion. The dog will associate word and action, and these will help it remember what you want done and when.

## The Meaning of "No"

When the puppy makes a mistake, use the word "no!" sharply so that it will learn the meaning. On the street, during an obedience lesson or training session, at home, or any time, always say "no!" in a sharp tone when your dog does the wrong thing. Your pet will soon understand what you mean.

## Collar and Leash

Let a puppy examine and smell a collar and leash before you use them. Place the collar around the puppy's neck and leave it there for a day before trying anything further. After the dog is used to the collar, snap on the leash and let the dog drag it around for a while, watching that the leash doesn't get tangled on something and frighten the dog. After the dog is used to the leash, take up your end of it and walk around with your pet, applying little or no pressure. Gradually, over a short period, increase your control until your dog learns that even though the leash is restraining, it is nothing to be afraid of.

Walk with your dog on the leash to your left. At first, a puppy will want to romp and pull ahead. Restrain your dog and, if it sits down, pet it, call it, and then start again. Snap lightly on the leash to persuade the dog to come along. Use only as much force as necessary to get the dog moving with you. Be patient; it may take awhile for your dog to get the idea that it is to walk with you.

You may want to use a training (choke) collar. The collar is of metal chain-links and has metal rings at each end. It forms a loop by slipping the chain through one of the rings; the other ring is where the leash is attached. The proper way to put on a choke collar is with the loose ring at the right of the dog's neck, the chain attached to it having come over the neck and through the holding ring rather than under the neck. A collar in this position will work correctly, as the dog is to be on your left during training.

Training collars allow you to exert as much or as little control as you need. You can get your dog's attention and encourage the proper behavior by giving a light, quick snap on the leash. This tightens the collar around the neck, but only for a moment. If you have put on the collar correctly, it will loosen instantly when pressure is released. Tug on the collar gently. Never use the training collar to place constant pressure on the dog's neck; this will choke the animal. In the right hands, a training collar can be a good training device, but in the wrong hands it can be dangerous and painful for a dog. Always remove the choke collar after the training session.

**The Great Dane has been properly trained to walk on a leash at its owner's left side.**

# The Basic Commands

Your dog should be under your control at all times. This means keeping your pet on a leash or in a fenced area when it's outside, and training it to respond to your commands. Dogs that are allowed to run loose or out of control turn over trash cans, cause traffic accidents, wreck gardens, dig up other people's yards, mess up sidewalks, and sometimes bite people.

**"Come."** Talk to your dog when you feed and play with it, and call it by name until your pet understands and responds. Fasten a long line to the collar, and let the dog play awhile. Say "come" and pull the dog all the way to you. Pet and feed it a little. Repeat this several times, using the rope less and less until the dog comes to you all the way, to be petted and rewarded.

Now try the command with the dog off the leash. Don't expect your pet to always respond when you are just starting. If the dog walks away from you, follow slowly and do not run. Bring the dog back to the starting place and start again with the leash.

**"Sit."** Have the dog on the leash to your left. Say "sit" and, at the same time, press the dog's rump into a sitting position. When the dog is seated to your satisfaction, give a bit of food and a word of praise. Repeat the lesson several times until the dog acts of its own accord.

Now have the dog sit, drop the leash, and walk away a few steps. Your pet probably will follow. Take the dog back to the starting place and repeat the exercise. Eventually you can teach a dog to remain seated until you give the command "come."

**"Down."** First get the dog to sit. Then say "down" and press the dog's shoulders down, at the same time pulling the front feet forward. Practice every day until your pet understands fully and will obey the command whether on or off the leash.

**"Stay."** Have the dog in the "down" position, and face your pet. Give the command "stay" and drop the leash. Raise your palm and back away. If the dog tries to follow, say "no" and hold your raised palm toward it. Put the dog back in position and repeat the training exercise until your pet will "stay" on command.

**"Heel."** You will need the chain type of training collar to teach this command. The goal is to have the dog walk at your left side at an even pace. Hold the end of the leash in your right hand, the training collar above the dog's neck in your left hand. The dog's chest should be kept next to your left leg. Pull your pet firmly into the proper place with your left hand as you walk along, and at the same time give the command "heel!" Praise the dog as long as it is in the right position. It should be taught to stop immediately when you stop and then to move forward when you move.

**"Take it," "drop it," and "get it."** Place a stick in the dog's mouth and say "take it." If the dog tries to drop it, replace the stick and hold it in, saying "take it." Then let the dog drop the stick, saying "drop it" as it falls so that the dog will associate the action with the command. When the dog learns to "take it," walk away a few steps and say "come," persuading the dog to carry the stick.

Take a ball and pretend to throw it. After a few tries, actually throw it a short distance and say "get it." When the dog picks it up, say "come." At the same time motion the dog to you, holding out your hand. Do not go after the ball; insist that your dog come all the way to you with it. Then give the command to "drop it."

## Correcting Bad Habits

**Jumping on furniture.** When your dog jumps on the bed or sofa or somewhere else it's not supposed to be, push your pet off the article, say "no!" sharply, and scold it.

**Jumping on people.** This annoying habit can be broken by raising your knee (and having your friends do the same) so that the dog is struck sharply on the chest as it jumps at you. Say "no!" at the same time you raise your knee.

**Barking.** Use the command "quiet!" if your dog barks excessively or late at night. Say "no!" and scold the dog to distract it from barking. Hold the mouth closed, repeating the commands "quiet" and "no."

There are times when a good watchdog ought to bark. Make sure, before you scold and correct your dog, that it doesn't hear something that justifies a warning bark.

**Car chasing.** If your dog comes when called, it may not get into this dangerous habit. If it does develop the habit, have a friend drive by, with someone in the car holding a pail of water to throw at the dog when it comes near the car. A large waterpistol will have the same effect. Soak the dog repeatedly, if necessary, until it learns to leave cars alone.

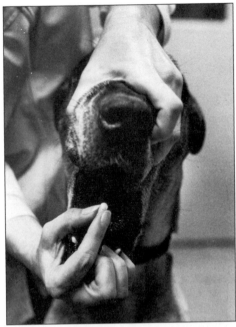

To give a pill, grasp the dog's muzzle, *left*, squeeze lips against teeth, and apply pressure just forward of the corners of the mouth. Place the tablet toward the base of the tongue. Close the mouth firmly, *below*. Massage the throat, lifting the muzzle up, to get the dog to swallow.

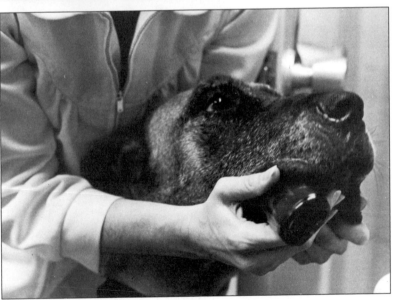

# Dog Illnesses

You don't want to take any chances with your dog's health. It pays to call in a professional if there is any doubt about what is wrong with your dog or what to do about it.

A dog cannot tell you how it feels. It takes many years of medical training and experience to know how to find out. Your nearby veterinarian can save a dog's life if called in time. Keep the phone number handy. Do not experiment with home remedies until it is too late.

## The Veterinarian's Job

Veterinarians study and treat diseases of animals, serve as advisers on matters relating to the care and breeding of animals, and inspect animal products for human consumption.

There are about 45,000 veterinarians in the United States. Most are specialists. They may specialize in the treatment of small animals, horses, livestock, or exotic animals. Most veterinarians are in private practice.

Soon after you get your dog you should have a veterinarian give it a thorough checkup. Prevention is better than cure. A veterinarian can tell you whether your dog needs worming or inoculations. A checkup will reveal external parasites that need removal or some other ailment that needs attention before it develops into a dangerous problem.

## Vaccinations

Your dog should be vaccinated against distemper, hepatitis, leptospirosis, parainfluenza ("kennel cough"), and parvovirus. These five vaccines usually are given as one shot. A puppy 6 to 8 weeks old should be taken to a veterinarian to receive its first shot, with the vaccination program to continue every 3 to 4 weeks thereafter until the dog is 12 to 16 weeks old. At 3 to 4 months of age, the dog should have a rabies shot, with yearly boosters thereafter.

These vaccinations are essential to your dog's good health. They will protect it from highly contagious diseases that can endanger its life. Even dogs that have little contact with other dogs need the protection of vaccinations, since these diseases can spread quickly even through indirect contact. Parvovirus, for instance, can be brought into the house on your shoes if you have walked through an infected area.

## External Parasites

Fleas, ticks, lice, and mites can make life miserable for your dog. Not only can they cause your dog great discomfort, they can carry disease. Fleas may carry tapeworm eggs. Ticks can carry blood parasites. Lice suck blood, and in great numbers can cause anemia. Mites cause mange. All parasites multiply incredibly fast.

You will know your dog has one of these parasites if you see it scratching furiously and biting into its coat. But you may not know which parasite is causing the problem. In general, it is best to let your veterinarian identify the pest and prescribe the proper powder, dip, or spray.

The best flea and tick control comes from dips—concentrated insecticide solutions that are diluted and applied to a dog when wet. After application, you must towel-dry the dog. Rinsing the dip off destroys its effectiveness. You may be able to buy dips from your veterinarian for home use, but in most cases your vet will dip the dog. It's important to treat your dog throughout the fall, since fleas do not die outside until the first frost of winter.

Commercial flea powders containing 10 percent sevin can be effective if dusted down to the skin and used once or twice a week. An aerosol spray makes it easier for you to get the medication all through the dog's coat, but you must be careful to keep the spray away from the eyes.

Flea shampoos also are effective but require you to bathe the dog frequently. They do not prevent fleas and ticks from reinfesting a dog.

The most popular flea-control products probably are flea collars, but their effectiveness is questionable, especially on large dogs.

Be sure any preparation you use is safe for dogs. Some preparations are unsafe for puppies or nursing dams. Some dips, powders, and sprays may be unsafe for cats.

It is essential that you eliminate the source of the parasite by cleaning out the doghouse, spraying it, and laundering bedding. The yard where your dog runs may be sprayed with an insecticide such as diazinon or pyrethrins to keep parasites away. Always follow label directions when using an insecticide for parasite control.

## Intestinal Worms

A veterinarian should check your dog for worms by examining a bowel movement sample for eggs. Worms can kill a puppy. If you have a puppy, have it examined for worms even if it doesn't show symptoms such as diarrhea, vomiting, and blood in the feces. You can't always detect the presence of worms by yourself; to be sure, have a veterinarian examine your dog.

Worming is best done by a vet since there are four kinds of intestinal worms (roundworms, hookworms, whipworms, and tapeworms), each calling for different treatment. Don't rely on over-the-counter wormers—they may be ineffective and even dangerous.

For the dog's protection and yours, keep its living quarters clean. Change drinking water often. Disinfect all feeding dishes, and be sure to rinse off all traces of disinfectant. Remove droppings from the dog's running area. Worms are persistent; you need to be persistent, too. Continue treatment until you are sure your dog is completely rid of the problem. These infestations seldom leave any lasting effects if treated promptly and completely.

## Heartworms

Heartworms are a serious problem in dogs, causing damage to the animal's heart, lungs, and liver. The parasites are transmitted by infected mosquitoes. Even dogs that are kept indoors most of the time can be bitten by a mosquito that carries the disease and thus be infected. Symptoms can include coughing, tiring easily upon exercise, fainting spells, poor appetite, and weight loss.

A veterinarian checking a dog for heartworms will take a blood sample and test it for evidence of the parasites. If heartworms are detected, treatment is long and difficult. A sick dog must be confined and kept quiet for weeks.

The problem is worse in wooded or marshy areas around lakes and ponds, where mosquitoes breed. Heartworms once were a major threat to the health of dogs mainly in the Gulf Coast states, but the problem has spread recently to the rest of the country.

Your veterinarian can prescribe a pill, tablet, or liquid medicine for you to give your dog to prevent infection. Many veterinarians feel that every dog should be on a heartworm prevention program. Ask your vet for information and recommendations.

## Skin Disorders

Daily care for your pet's coat will go a long way toward helping avoid the many diseases that affect a dog's skin.

Because many skin disorders have symptoms in common, do not try to diagnose your dog's ailment and treat it. You may make matters worse.

When you see worn patches on the coat, pimples, inflammation, or rash, take your dog to the veterinarian for a diagnosis. The cause of the skin problem can be one of a number of things: external parasites, allergy, and mange are only a few.

## When Your Dog Is Ill

If your dog gets sick, don't just trust nature to take care of the problem. You may cause your pet needless suffering. Instead, call your veterinarian right away. If the illness occurs after office hours and you do not have your veterinarian's home telephone number (it is wise to keep this handy at all times), look in the phone book for an emergency veterinary service. Many cities have one.

Don't give your dog a medicine that was meant for people unless your vet has approved its use. Some human remedies can be harmful for animals.

### How Do You Know When a Dog Is Ill?

Among veterinarians and breeders, the term "thrifty" indicates a vibrant or lively dog, and "unthrifty" a listless, lazy dog. When it's ill, a dog will lose its pep and its coat and eyes may become dull. It may be indifferent to food and it may vomit and have diarrhea. The eyes and nose may be runny. The nose may or may not be cold. Contrary to popular belief, the temperature of a dog's nose is no sure sign of either health or illness.

### Taking Temperature

It's not difficult to take a dog's temperature, and your pet won't mind it (much). Use an ordinary rectal thermometer, lubricated with petroleum jelly. Insert half its length into the dog's rectum for 2 minutes. Average temperature is 101.5°.

### Caring for the Sick Dog

If your family life is already busy, it may be best to leave a sick dog in an animal hospital for treatment. Caring for it would take a great deal of time as well as love. However, if your dog will pine for you, it may recover faster at home.

Your dog needs rest when it is ill but, like a small child, it often does not have the sense to stay quiet. It is up to you to restrict your pet's activity. Put your dog in an isolated room or corner where it is warm and not drafty. If the weather is bad, you may not want the dog to go outside, so put newspapers in the sickroom.

Check temperature, breathing, bowel movements, appetite, urination, nasal discharge, and vomiting daily to help you accurately describe your dog's progress to your veterinarian.

## Keeping the Patient Clean

If your dog is well enough to go outdoors to evacuate, or can use the newspapers in the sickroom, your problem is not difficult. If your dog goes outdoors, be sure to wipe off its feet when it returns so that dirt won't wind up in the sickbed.

If the dog is too weak to get up, cover the bed with easily washed small towels or clean paper. A small towel also can serve as a diaper, if necessary. If the dog is paralyzed or so weak that it cannot move easily, turn it over often to prevent bedsores. Long-haired dogs that are immobilized for any length of time should be clipped around the hindquarters and other contact areas.

## Giving Medicines

Follow directions exactly when administering medicines. If your veterinarian prescribes medication for certain times, that's when it must be given. You cannot skip one time and give a double dose the next.

If the dog's medicine is not bad-tasting, you may be able to administer it easily by mixing it with food or liquids. But your dog's very sensitive nose may at once detect a foreign scent in the food. If the dog won't take medicine with food and won't open its mouth and swallow medicine willingly, here's what to do.

**Pills.** Butter the pill to make it slippery. Grasp the dog's muzzle, squeeze lips against teeth, and apply pressure just forward of the corners of the mouth. Push lips between teeth. (If the dog gets rough, it will bite itself.) Tilt the head backward. Place, don't throw, the tablet toward the base of the tongue. Close the mouth firmly, then massage the throat, lifting the muzzle up. The dog will have no choice but to swallow.

**Liquids.** Grasp the lower lip in front of the corner of the mouth and pull it out gently to form a pouch. Pour medicine, preferably from a small bottle, into the pouch a little at a time, then close the pouch and let the dog swallow. If you lift the muzzle up, the dog has little choice but to let the medicine run through clenched teeth and down its throat.

Be firm, but kind and gentle. The dog will soon see that you mean business and that it is useless to resist.

**Caution:** Do not throw either liquids or pills down the dog's throat. They could enter the windpipe and cause the dog to choke.

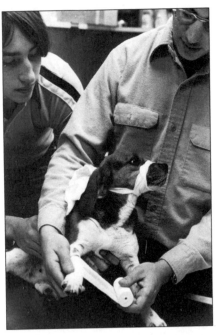

Muzzle a dog before giving first aid, *left,* unless it is choking or vomiting. Follow a veterinarian's instructions when treating your pet.

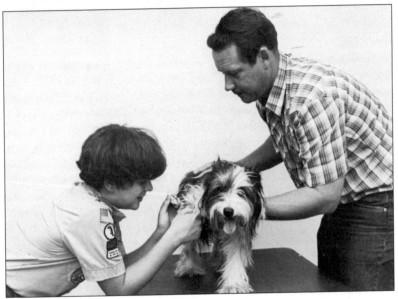

# In Case of Accident

You can help keep your dog safe by checking your home to be sure that household chemicals, automotive supplies, paints, lead drapery weights, garden pesticides and fertilizers, and similar threats are out of your dog's reach. When you're away from home, unplug electrical cords in your dog's confinement area and make sure there's no potential danger to your pet from items that are sharp or small enough to be swallowed. Never let your dog run free or chase cars; build a fence around the yard and walk your dog only on a leash. Preventive care like this will protect your pet from many common accidents.

When an emergency does arise, however, you must know what to do to help your dog. Learn first aid skills and proper emergency procedures. Keep telephone numbers for the veterinarian, pet emergency center, and poison control center by the phone and in your wallet. Be prepared to act quickly, calmly, and sensibly if your dog is involved in an accident.

## First Aid

It's crucial to save time in an emergency. In general, don't try to treat the dog yourself if you are near an animal hospital or pet emergency clinic. If there's severe bleeding or other life-threatening injury, however, or you're miles from a veterinarian, you will have to give first aid.

Imagine a common accident: Your dog runs into a busy street and is struck by a car. What should you do?

Get a passerby to stand near you and wave a handkerchief to flag down traffic while you assess the dog's condition. A seriously injured dog is frightened and in pain, and may attempt to bite even its owner. Before you begin first aid, muzzle the dog with a long strip of gauze, a necktie, belt, two handkerchiefs, or a soft rope. Approach slowly and quietly, speaking in a comforting tone. Tie a loop of gauze two-thirds of the way from nose tip to jaw. Knot the loop securely on top, then again below the nose, and tie the ends of the strip behind the dog's head to keep the frightened animal from scratching the muzzle off. *Do not muzzle a dog that is vomiting or choking.*

Get the dog to a veterinarian at once. If there's severe bleeding or the dog's breathing or heart has stopped, treat as follows to stabilize the animal's condition, then rush the victim to a vet.

**Proper application of an emergency muzzle**

## Bleeding

Direct pressure by hand can halt almost all severe bleeding. Use a clean cloth and apply direct, constant pressure to the wound. If you have a first aid kit, place a gauze pad over the wound, use gauze strips to wrap it tightly, and tie or tape the ends. Use a tourniquet only as a last resort.

**To stop bleeding, apply direct pressure, then place gauze on the wound and secure it in place.**

To make a tourniquet, wrap gauze, fabric, or rope twice around the wounded leg, between the heart and the wound, and knot it. Do not make the tourniquet too tight. Get the dog to a veterinarian immediately. A tourniquet can cause loss of the leg or nerve damage if left in place too long. If medical help is more than 15 or 20 minutes away, loosen the tourniquet every 5 minutes.

## CPR

If the dog's heart has stopped you must administer cardiopulmonary

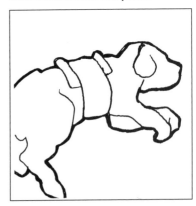

resuscitation. Place the heel of one hand on the dog's chest and put your other hand palm-down on the first. Press firmly, release, pause, and repeat 20 or 30 times a minute until the heartbeat resumes. Take into account the dog's size — don't bruise or break the ribs.

**Take care not to injure the dog when administering CPR.**

### Transportation

Don't let an injured dog walk or run. Quiet the animal as much as you can, and cover with a blanket or other warm cloth.

A dog that has been hit by a car or has broken bones must be moved carefully. Gently slide the dog onto an ironing board, blanket, jacket, or other makeshift stretcher. If you can't make a stretcher, carry the animal carefully in your arms. Support a small dog in the crook of your arm with your hand held under the chest. Hold a larger dog across your arms, with each arm just inside a pair of legs.

Get the dog to a veterinarian as soon as possible.

## Other Common Emergencies

**Allergic reactions.** Symptoms include runny eyes, sneezing, severe itch, swelling of eyes and face, and even unconsciousness. Call your veterinarian.

**Bites, cat or dog.** Clean the wounds with Betadine soap or solution. Take the dog to a veterinarian. If your dog is bitten by a stray dog or a wild animal such as a skunk and you suspect rabies, get professional advice at once.

**Chemical burns.** Flush the skin with water for 10 to 15 minutes. Treat internal burns as poisoning.

**Other burns.** Do not apply anything to burns. Cover the area with a clean, dry cloth and rush the dog to your veterinarian.

**Choking.** Push lower jaw open and tilt the head up. Very carefully try to remove the object with your fingers. If that doesn't work, kneel behind the dog, holding its body just below the ribs. Squeeze hard a few times, pressing up. If the object does not pop out, get to a veterinarian.

**Convulsions and seizures.** Try to restrain the dog until the convulsion or seizure is over so that it won't hurt itself. See a veterinarian at once.

**Drowning.** Hold the dog upside down for 10 to 15 seconds. Give artifical respiration and, if there's no heartbeat, CPR. Wrap the dog warmly.

**Electric shock.** Knock the electrical cord out of the socket with a wooden object. Give CPR and artifical respiration. Keep the dog warm.

**Fractures.** Restrict the dog's movement. Do not attempt to set the bone. If you are far from a veterinarian, wrap the limb with cotton; splint front legs or upper back legs with a stick, rolled newspaper, or similar object; and wrap loosely with gauze. Get the dog to a vet as soon as possible.

**Frostbite.** Take the dog to a warm place. Do not rub with snow or ice.

**Heatstroke, heat prostration.** Symptoms include panting, vomiting, rapid pulse, staggering, high fever (105° to 107°F), and collapse. Lower the dog's body temperature by hosing or immersing the animal in cool water up to the neck for 10 minutes. Apply an ice pack to the head.

**Poisoning.** If your dog has swallowed poison and you know what it was, your veterinarian may recommend an antidote or tell you to induce vomiting with a hydrogen peroxide solution, syrup of ipecac, or other emetic. With some poisons, however, it's dangerous to induce vomiting. If you can't contact a medical expert, give the dog activated charcoal, milk, egg whites, or milk of magnesia to help absorb the poison.

**Shock.** The symptoms include pale gums, blue tongue, and rapid, shallow breathing. Keep the dog warm and quiet. Do not give fluids if there may be internal injuries, or if the animal is vomiting or having convulsions.

**Snakebite.** Do not let the dog walk. Carry it to a veterinarian immediately.

**Swallowed objects.** If the dog has swallowed a soft object such as a rubber ball or a hard and smooth small object such as a marble, induce vomiting. Do not induce vomiting of sharp objects.

## Get Professional Help

Once you've taken emergency action to help the injured dog, it's vital that you take the animal to a veterinarian immediately. There may be internal injuries that aren't readily apparent. You can handle minor problems yourself, but if your dog is in pain, you don't know what's wrong, you don't know the proper treatment, or there's any doubt about the seriousness of an injury or accident, don't take chances. Consult your veterinarian.

Long before you need to know, it's a good idea to ask your veterinarian, "What would you like me to do in case of an emergency?" Find out if your vet will meet you at the clinic if an emergency arises at night or on a weekend. Find out if the vet makes house calls. Locate the nearest pet emergency center and find out what hours it is open. If your community has a poison control center or hotline, make a note of the telephone number and carry it with you. If your emergency preparations are thorough, you'll feel more confident about handling the situation properly should your dog be injured.

## Non-Emergency Treatment

The most common injuries you'll treat probably will be small cuts and bite wounds. These superficial cuts and wounds are treated just like any other wound. Clean them with Betadine, and bandage with clean gauze, if needed.

Relieve the pain of superficial burns with ice cubes or cold water. Gently dry the affected area and apply a burn ointment. Do not use any greases, ointments, or other first aid burn remedies on extensive burns. Cover with a clean, dry dressing and see a veterinarian.

For constipation, give milk of magnesia, 1 teaspoon for every 10 pounds of body weight. Do not give any other laxatives intended for people. Do not give milk of magnesia if you suspect the trouble is caused by a swallowed object.

For diarrhea, give Kaopectate, 1 teaspoon per 10 pounds of body weight. Feed unseasoned cooked starches, eggs, rice, cottage cheese, mashed potatoes, small amounts of lean meat. Do not give milk.

If your dog gets into poison ivy, it probably will not affect the dog, only the people who touch the poison on its coat. Wearing rubber gloves, wash your pet with a mild soap.

A minor eye irritation may be relieved by rinsing with a piece of water-soaked cotton. Call a veterinarian if an eye injury is serious.

If your dog tangles with a porcupine and gets stuck with a few quills, apply a muzzle, cut the quills with scissors, and ease them out carefully with tweezers or needlenose pliers. Treat as for puncture wounds. If there are many quills, take the dog to a veterinarian immediately to have them removed under anesthesia.

To remove skunk odor, wash the dog in tomato juice, followed by soap and water. Then rinse with a solution of vanilla extract.

## Emergency Supplies to Have on Hand

Much of what you'll need is already in your home medicine cabinet. Items to have handy include:

Tweezers, for removal of splinters or glass
Rectal thermometer
Petroleum jelly, to lubricate the thermometer
Eyedropper (plastic), for giving liquid medicine or antidotes
Sterile cotton
Gauze bandage, in rolls, for wounds and for muzzling an injured dog
Gauze pads, to protect wounds and burns and control bleeding
Adhesive tape, for bandages
Blunt-ended scissors
Betadine scrub and ointment, an antiseptic, for cleaning and dressing
    wounds
Hydrogen peroxide, 3 percent solution, to clean wounds and induce
    vomiting
Activated charcoal, to absorb poison
Syrup of ipecac, to induce vomiting
Mineral oil or milk of magnesia (laxatives)
Kaopectate (for diarrhea)
Rubbing alcohol, a disinfectant

It is wise to consult your veterinarian before giving any medication or treatment.

# Dogs and the Law

Since there are more than 50 million dogs in the United States, laws have been enacted in every state to regulate their registration, control, and humane treatment. These laws vary greatly from state to state and from city to city. In most places, collars, rabies tags, and municipal licenses are required for dogs. You can get information on applicable laws from various sources, depending on whether you live on a farm, in a small town, or in a big city. Try these:

City clerk
Police department
SPCA or humane society
The American Kennel Club
Farm bureau secretary
Your veterinarian

## In Case of Dogbite

Though rabies is not as common today as it once was, thanks to the laws requiring vaccination of dogs and cats, it is still possible to get rabies from a dogbite. Infection and tetanus also are of concern. Take the following steps in case of dogbite.

1. Wash the wound thoroughly with soap and water.
2. See a physician immediately.
3. Report the bite to the city or county public health department. This is the law in most states. Health department officials will contact the owner of the dog and make sure the animal has been vaccinated against rabies. If the dog has not had a rabies shot within the year, it will be quarantined until health officials are sure it does not have the disease.

# Books About Dog Care

American Kennel Club. *The Complete Dog Book: The Official Publication of the American Kennel Club.* 16th ed. Howell Books, 1979.

Kirk, Robert W. *First Aid for Pets: The Pet Owner's Complete Guide to Emergency Care of Dogs, Cats and Other Small Animals.* Dutton, 1978.

Mars, Charlotte. *A Guide to Raising Your Dog Successfully.* Rosen, 1978.

McGinnis, Terri. *The Well Dog Book.* Random, 1974.

*Nutrient Requirements of Dogs.* Committee on Animal Nutrition, National Academy of Sciences. National Academy Press, 1975.

Pinkwater, Jill. *Superpuppy: How to Choose, Raise, and Train the Best Possible Dog for You.* Houghton, 1976.

Unkelbach, Kurt. *How to Bring Up Your Pet Dog.* Dodd, 1972.

Unkelbach, Kurt. *How to Teach an Old Dog New Tricks.* Dodd, 1979.

## Pamphlets

You may find these publications at your veterinarian's office; or write Pet Information Center, 505 Market Street, Knoxville, TN 37902, for information on obtaining copies.

*Caring for the Older Dog*
*Getting Rid of Parasites*
*Grooming for Good Health*
*Preventing and Handling Common Emergencies*
*Raising the Sporting Dog*
*Teaching Your Child About Dogs*
*What You Should Know About Neutering*
*Why and When Your Dog Needs Vaccinations*

Many of the major drug companies, pet food manufacturers, and other organizations publish literature on the care and feeding of animals. Many of these publications have excellent sections on health and diseases. These are usually free. You may write to the following companies and organizations for information on obtaining copies.

Allied Mills Research Center, 110 North Wacker Drive, Chicago, IL 60606.

American Veterinary Medical Association, 930 North Meacham Road, Schaumberg, IL 60196.

Animal Welfare Institute, P.O. Box 3650, Washington, DC 20007.

Borden Chemical Division, 180 East Broad Street, Columbus, OH 43215.

Carnation Company, 5045 Wilshire Boulevard, Los Angelos, CA 90036.

Gaines Dog Research Center, 250 North Street, White Plains, NY 10625.

Ralston Purina Company, Checkerboard Square, St. Louis, MO 63188.

Shell Chemical Company, One Shell Plaza, P.O. Box 2463, Houston, TX 77001.

Swift and Company, Pet Food Products, 115 West Jackson Boulevard, Chicago, IL 60604.

## Magazines

*Canine Chronicle.* Routledge Publications, Inc., Box 115, Montpelier, IN 47359. For those who breed and show purebred dogs.

*Dog Fancy.* Fancy Publications, Inc., Box 4030, San Clemente, CA 92672. Covers all phases of dog ownership.

*Dog World.* 300 West Adams Street, Chicago, IL 60606. For purebred dog breeders, kennel owners, and shows exhibitors.

*Pure-Bred Dogs—American Kennel Gazette.* American Kennel Club, Inc., 51 Madison Avenue, New York, NY 10010. For purebred dog breeders and owners.

## Boy Scout Literature

*Pets* and *Veterinary Science* merit badge pamphlets

# Acknowledgments

The Boy Scouts of America is grateful to the following individuals for their assistance in preparing this revised edition of the *Dog Care* merit badge pamphlet: John Mandeville, director of Public Communication and Education, American Kennel Club; Dr. Alice M. Wolf, Department of Small Animal Medicine and Surgery, College of Veterinary Medicine, Texas A&M University; James E. Schroeder, DVM; Charles Robert Hart, DVM; H. W. Weicht, DVM; Guy Hodge, director of Data and Information Services, Humane Society of the United States; and Deborah L. Sizemore, science and agricultural writer.

The Boy Scouts of America also is grateful to the following organizations and individuals for their assistance in preparing the 1972 revision of the *Dog Care* merit badge pamphlet, much of which is included in the new edition: J. Thomas Johnson, DVM; American Kennel Club; American Museum of Natural History; J. Stuart Crawford, DVM; *LIFE* magazine (illustrations); Edwin Megargee, artist, for original drawings of breeds of dogs for *LIFE* magazine; Paul Brown, artist, for sketches of parts of a dog; Lois Stevenson; Emil Brodbeck; Fred Keesing; Jack Pelletier; John Dominis; ASPCA of New York; Frank W. Kingsbury, DVM, extension veterinarian, Rutgers, The State University of New Jersey; and members of Veterinary Science Explorer Post 601, Allen Products, Allentown, Pennsylvania, for staging, taking, and providing special photographs.